Echoes of an Asylum

Gautham Shaji

Presentation by *BookLeaf Publishing*

Web: www.bookleafpub.com

E-mail: info@bookleafpub.com

ISBN: 9789360949921

First edition 2024

ACKNOWLEDGEMENT

I would like to give a special thanks to my sister, Gopika, for always being my support and my parents, this book would not be possible without you. I would also like to thank my best friend, Arya, for helping me reach where I am and Laura, who helped me with editing and naming of the book and for constantly being a guiding light.

Relapse

Freefalling

I could feel the air burning my lungs
With every breath I took, free falling;
Free falling into oblivion or remembrance?
All I remember was my desolation but there she
was,
Every breath I took was in yearning for her,
And yet like the stars she could never
Be touched, be felt, only to be seen
Millions of miles away.
My only memories were of me falling
Free falling into her, into an endless depth
With never an end in sight, but now
All I can feel is my breath, burning my lungs.

Suffocation

The hues of the setting sun
Gave an orange tint to the ocean
The clouds took on the colour of the sun
In reverence or maybe in mourning;
The water feels so cold,
The birds were seen dancing to their own music
A solitary fishing boat was rocking and weaving,
Witnessing the spectacle unfold.
The water feels so heavy;
The silence, broken by the crashing of the waves
Or the gushing of the wind
Bringing the scent of the stories,
Hidden deep under the ocean
The water feels so fine
I can hardly brea—

Cigarettes

Lit my first cigarette of the day
The melancholic smoke filling my lungs
The pungent aroma dissipated through the air
Anything... anything to forget her scent
For me it was euphoric
To see which addiction of mine would kill me
first
the sunlight peering through the smoke
I feel the burning sensation
Killing me ever so slowly
Inch by inch
I hoped as it killed me it would also kill
This desolation, this despair
I extinguished the memories underneath my foot
And lit another one.

Shell Shock

The eerie dark, stench of rotting bodies
The dirt in my boots and shirt
Pricking my skin,
The silence broken by
Sound of gunfire in the distance and
Mice, eating to their hearts' content
The mutilated bodies of comrades.
The metallic body of my rifle being
My only anchor to reality
Sound of footsteps fast approaching
I hold my gun close to my chest
Swallow the desire to scream
The sound gets closer
I can hardly breathe
Over there! Two faces!
Hidden in the night
Panting, huffing, scrambling

I aim and shoot, the gun is jammed
Fear taking hold, the faces coming closer
I take out my knife and lunge at them
The blood of my enemies spurt across my face
"Daddy!" I hear my daughter's wail
When I came to, the lifeless bodies of
My wife and daughter lying
On the floor of my bedroom
Alas! The battlefield had come home with me.

Light

Crawling on all fours, slowly climbing my way up
The weight of gravity bearing down upon me
Each step forward, harder than the last
Only thing audible was the deafening silence
Enveloped by the chilling grip of darkness
A burst of light, so bright that it was blinding
Its warmth only searing;
Bewitching, persuading me to leap into its
embrace
There I was, without a second thought,
Airborne like a moth to the flame
The ice in my heart melting away
My feet no longer burdened by the callous
ground
As I opened my eyes, the familiar chill took hold
And all I could see, weightless and floating
Was the neverending darkness forevermore.

Walls

They say the road to hell

Is paved with good intentions,

But the way to my heart is

Blocked from your view

With each brick so meticulously

And with such attention to detail

Placed to build a wall so high.

It has caged me inside

I cannot climb or fly

I would like to build you a door

But I don't know how.

So I hope one day you will

Siege through this wall

But my biggest fear is

If you do reach me,

You would be everything to me

But would I be just a ditch

To quench your loneliness

Or just one option of countless many?

Would you truly miss me

If I was ever gone?

Flight

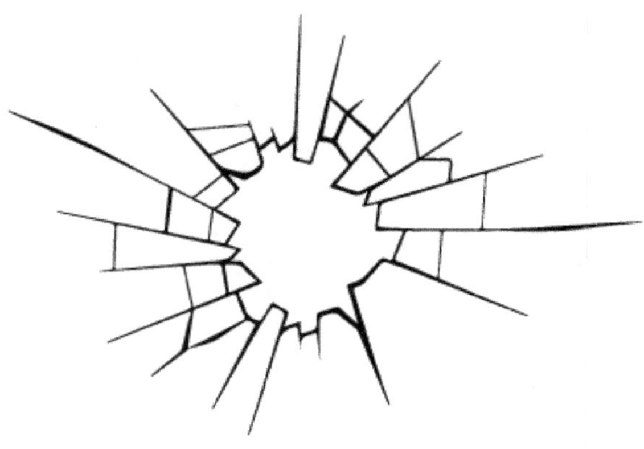

I stood there on the parapet of the roof
Looking down at the ground so far below me.
Holding onto the railings
Just a wind's graze, to escape Fate's clutch
I stood there for a moment my heavy thoughts
Fading away; replaced by hollowness
Where my heart used to be
Reminding me
Of the countless times I've died inside;
Now here I was ready to fly
No angels or demons or God to save me
I remembered the happy faces
Of my mother urging me on,
All my friends cheering for me
How my dad, when I was little,
Threw me in the air and caught me
But here I was, falling, ready to feel his embrace
But there was no one there to catch me.

Rebirth

Would You Be So Kind

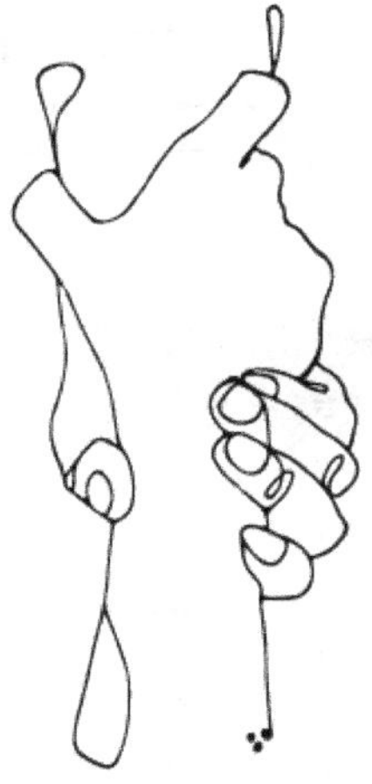

Would you be so kind as to
Free me from my own expectations,
Because I'm trapped between
The place I am and the place I want to be.
Would you be so kind as to
Help me find the real me;
Would you run away in fear?
Or would you be bored of who you find?
Would you be so kind as to
Find the key for this cage I'm in
Because all I can do is observe
But not touch or feel the world outside
I've been here forever
In a world devoid of life or colour
Am I asking too much when I ask you
To be kind to someone like me?

Art

"There he goes again," the asylum guard
exclaims
On his computer screen, the footage of
A pale old man etching lines on the walls
Of his room, with just his bare nails
The old man suddenly collapses,
The guards run in to save the dying man
His fingers bleeding from constant scraping
Of nonsensical lines on his asylum walls.
But the old man drew his last breath
With a smile on his face.

The next tenant, a quintessential
Artist gone mad, brought in writhing and
struggling
Looked at the lines in wonder.
He calmly pondered over the markings
And started scribbling on a piece of paper.
When the night shift guard peeked at the
drawing
He saw a portrait of a beautiful woman
"That cannot possibly be! This drawing—
It's the picture of the old man's deceased
daughter."

The Man in Search of Love

There once lived a man in a land far away
Who went on a quest to find a lost treasure.
He would search for it in the tallest of peaks
He would search for it in the deepest of oceans
But he could never find this wonder.
Till he met a wise old sage that said,
"That which you seek can be found
In the garden of roses to the west."
The man braved the elements,
He braved the foul beasts,
He braved the thorns,
And the traps and the night.
Till he, at last, found the chest that contained the treasure
Only to find it was empty, with a note that read,
"That which you seek would never have been yours."
The man finally understood.
He built a small house in the Garden
And lived with the sight and smell and touch
Of the Roses, finally content.

Warrior

"Hey boy, your anger scorches the earth
Melting the hearts of those around you,
Spitting words weaved to be more vile
Than the sting of a hundred bullet ants.
Hey boy, why are you so angry
Do you believe your warrior blood
Makes you privy to the secrets of the world?
Your father's money or your uncle's influence
Grants you the will fit for a king?
My boy, you who have achieved nothing
Nothing of value to show for
Nothing that has the power to inspire a soul
Who throws tantrums at the unfair whims of fate

While you trample on all those who love you.
Come my boy, and sit beside me
Share with me this cigarette and warm cup of tea
Enjoy the grand exodus of the beautiful sun,
For the world moves for men far greater than
you."

A Date with Lady Love

The blue moon stood solitary against the night
sky,
Its radiant light illuminating the path forward.
My carriage slowly trudges the barren road
There in the distance stood my date, Lady Love
"Why is love afraid of me?" I inquired,
As she gracefully got onto my carriage.
"Wherever I search for love it's never there
So love must be afraid of me." Lady Love
Gave a smile, to the envy of the moon,
"My dear, you have always searched for love
In places you knew it could never be found.
Your penchant for suffering has led you
On a trail of chasing heartbreaks.
You can't even dream of a world with
Someone that can ever love or care for you
My dear, Love was never afraid of you,

You were afraid of Love. That is your curse
To forever be numb to the Love you receive
To gasp for air in a garden of sunflowers."

Meaning

Gazing at eternity, through a glass window
The never-ending night sky looming
Over us; tiny specks of stardust.
"What is the meaning of life?"
The question was puzzling for her.
"What do you mean?" her eyes
Transfixed on distant galaxies.
"We whisper our sorrows into
Pocket dimension hoping to find
The purpose of our actions.
Be it the futility of Sisyphus
Or the enlightenment of suffering,
The pursuit of vanity or the almighty,
Why do you think we are here?"
She gave a smile, "Well I don't know all that
But we are here, aren't we?
So why not stay here a bit longer."
I felt all my existence converging
To that one moment in time.

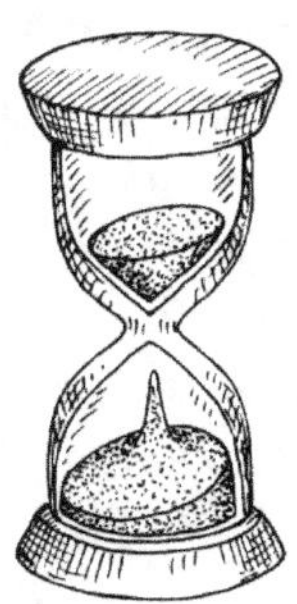

Mortals

A cold hand grasped my shoulder
As I watched the burning pyre.
"He was gone too soon."
The smoke burning my eyes
"We try and find meaning in Death
The most cold, callous;
The most random event in our life.
This existence is but fleeting, transitory
Forgotten just like smoke to the flames.
Yet we burn them to the ground
Jump into their cinders,
Their ashes clinging to us
Never to be washed away.
The warmth from this flame
Guiding us to a better future.
There may yet be a meaning,
That eludes us, to all of this."
"Come then, it is time." It said.

Recovery

Closure

Your eyes remind me of the night sky
Studded with stars, nebulae
And other heavenly bodies
Of cosmic significance.
Yet when I peer into your eyes
In the infinite possibilities I could see
I was but insignificant in the end.
So I move on like nothing ever happened.

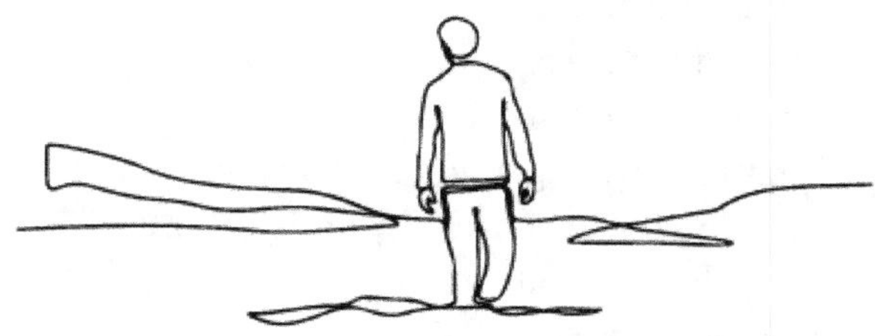

Dear Old Friend

Dear Old Friend,
Where do I even start, even though;
We are millions of miles apart.
They say life is a multitude
Of chance encounters and I am glad
We conquered the infinitesimally small
Probability of meeting each other.
For you were the only one willing
To brave the blizzard, and
Thaw out the ice of a frostbitten man.
Only you could bore through
My hatred, my anger and my sorrow.
So if ever you feel unworthy or dejected
Feel useless or apathetic,
Just know there is one life
That is eternally grateful to you.
Yours lovingly.

Language

My father is a man of few words
But all the words in the world
Fail to express the joy I see
When I reach home safe and sound.
My mother would often get cross over,
My unkept room, my eating habits,
And my questionable dressing sense
Yet each word of anger and irritation uttered
Hides a world unsaid between each line.
My friends would never even whisper
A kind word to my face, but I prefer that
Over the sweet words of a heartless man.
For each prayer that echoes
Within the hospital wall, For each
Kiss goodbye at the airport terminal
For each Rupee you pay for
A stranger in the bus, lies Something
That mere mixture of alphabets cannot fathom,

The progenitor of Language. We often seek
For a certain someone to understand our
anguish,
Even without us speaking.
But if one looks around, they can feel
The unspoken language in the
Multiple mundane things done for us.

Soul

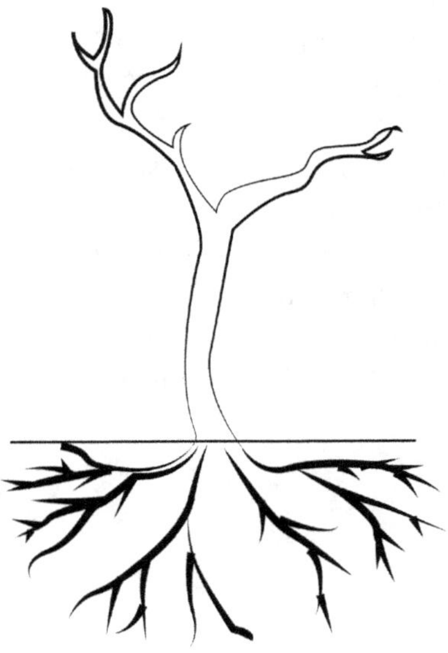

I peek through my office window, at a young
woman
Slowly shuffling her way and
Emptying a bottle of water under a tree.
Every single day come rain or shine
She would be there with her bottle of water.
The tree at first glance looked naught;
Of any import or uniqueness.
Vines festoon its trunk and branches
Under its shade grew numerous
Fragrant hyacinths of red, black and purple
The chirping of the birds and the buzzing of the
bees

That made homes on the boughs
Fill my eardrums with joy.
The floor was littered with half-eaten fruits
Which may get replaced by a flower or a tree
That would grow and blossom in its place.
Teardrops trace her freckled skin as she left
Inching closer I lay eyes
On the bark, engraved with the words,
"Here lies Adam, a loving father."
Irony must be a cruel mistress
That only in death do we truly love.

Poet

A poet's life, my dear, is filled with
A mixture of metaphors and misery.
You never know the point where
Their metaphors end and their misery begins.
Their sweetest dreams are but naught
The worst nightmare of you and I;
The void in the space where
Their heart used to be,
Compels them to pick up their weapon
And fight for their life on a piece of paper.
But for me something else pushes me;
What drives me isn't hope or pain
It's the rage buried deep within me
No poor soul can peer and see the fire
That burns in me everyday.
And so I write hoping, praying
That one day, I can quench this—
This insatiable fury in me
Lest the inferno consumes me whole.

The Door

The sterile smell of the Room
Matched with the bland white walls
Perfectly symbolises my prison.
All day spent staring at the Door
The Door to the outside.
The voices in my head telling me
That the Door would never open
For someone like me.
Everyday I would bang at the door
Hoping someone would open it.
But the efforts were futile.
No one came.
I mustered up my courage and
Turned the handle. Lo and Behold!
The Door swung wide open.

Yesterday

As the autumn leaves fell, slowly brushing the
face
Of a sprightly young man, all dressed up.
On his face you could see, a hopeful smile
As he touched the bark of this age-old tree.
The rough tree trunk reminded him of the time
He would climb its meandering branches,
The smell of the dead autumn leaves
Brought him back to his first heartbreak,
As he wept underneath its cool shade.
But just as these memories have come and gone
This moment too shall be lost to the banality of
time
And tomorrow shall come bringing with it,
Its fair share of winter and spring.
The world of yesterdays had faded long ago
Its remnants and pieces fitting to form today.